VOCAL SELECTIONS

Barry Manilow's COPACABANA
THE MUSICAL

Barry Manilow is a registered trademark of Hastings/Clayton/Tucker, Inc.

ISBN 0-634-02268-7

HAL•LEONARD®
CORPORATION

7777 W. BLUEMOUND RD. P.O. BOX 13819 MILWAUKEE, WI 53213

Visit Hal Leonard Online at
www.halleonard.com

JUST ARRIVED

Music by BARRY MANILOW
Lyric by BRUCE SUSSMAN and JACK FELDMAN

just ar - rived! _____

just ar - rived! _____

LOLA: Hey world, I've

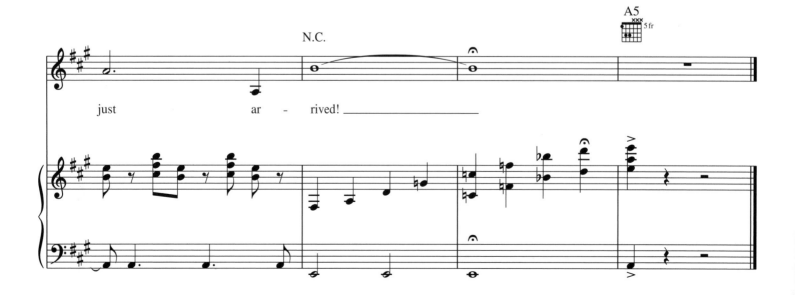

just ar - rived! _____

DANCIN' FOOL

Music by BARRY MANILOW
Lyric by BRUCE SUSSMAN and JACK FELDMAN

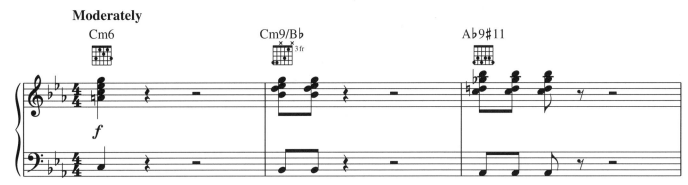

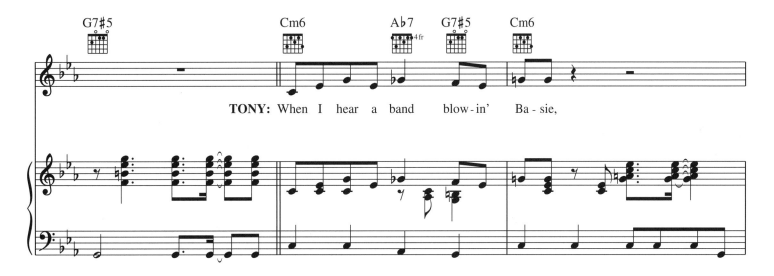

TONY: When I hear a band blow-in' Ba - sie,

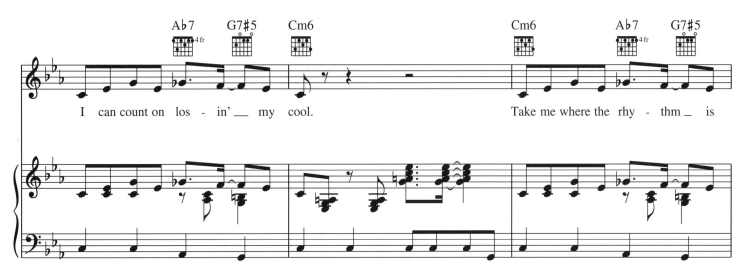

I can count on los - in' __ my cool.

Take me where the rhy - thm __ is

SWEET HEAVEN
(I'm in Love Again)

Music by BARRY MANILOW
Lyric by BRUCE SUSSMAN and JACK FELDMAN

Moderate Swing feel

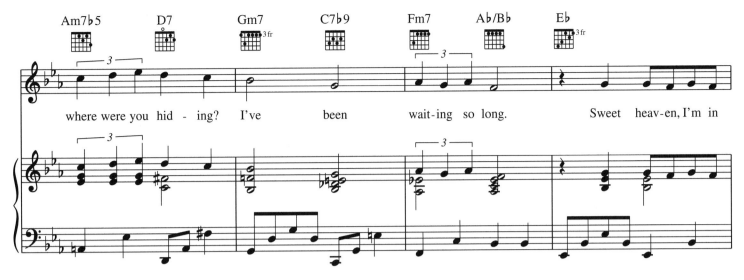

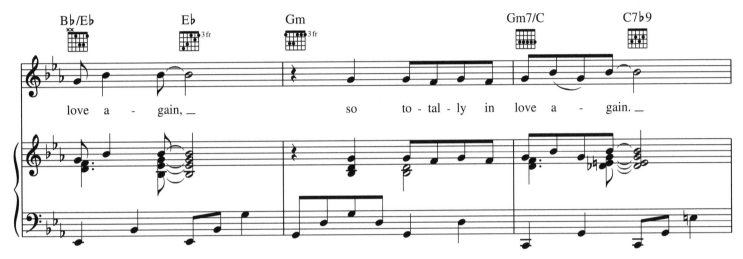

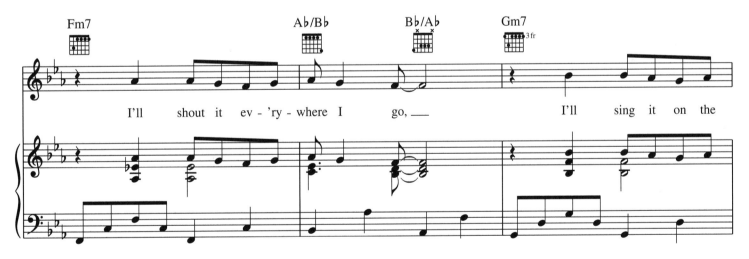

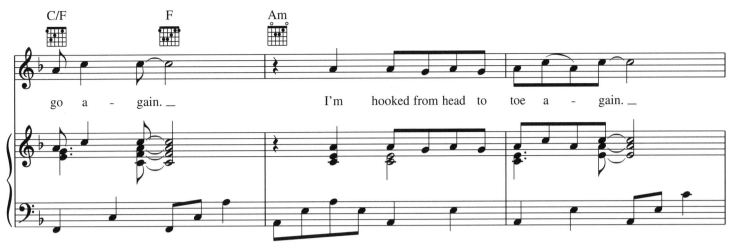

go a - gain. ___ I'm hooked from head to toe a - gain. ___

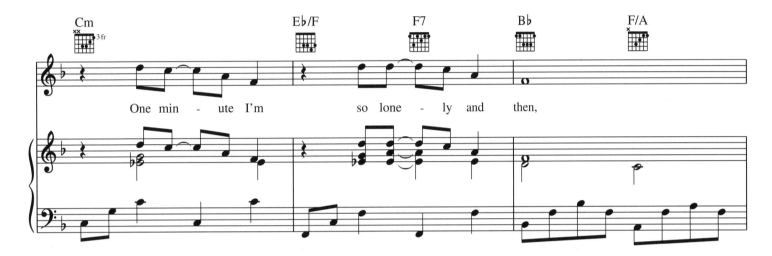

One min - ute I'm so lone - ly and then,

oh, heav - en! Hey! Babe! Now that I've found ___ you,

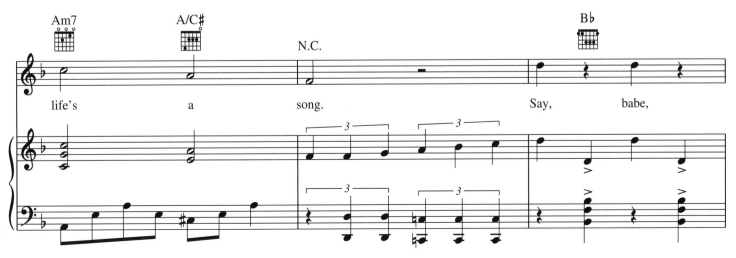

life's a song. Say, babe,

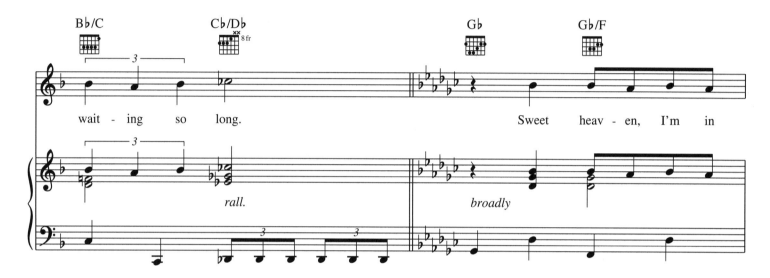

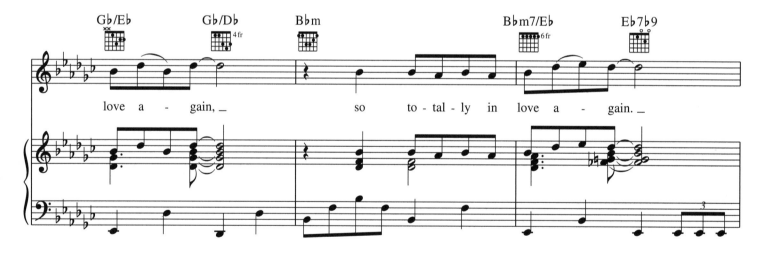

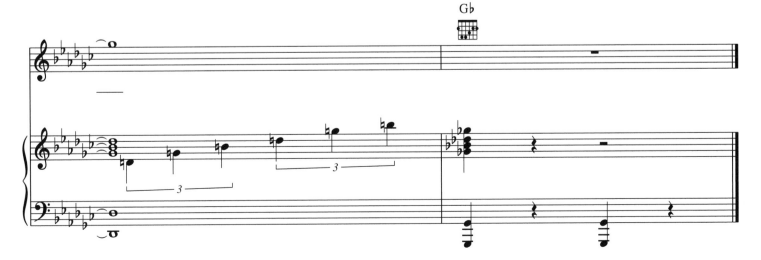

WHEN YOU'RE A COPA GIRL

Music by BARRY MANILOW
Lyric by BRUCE SUSSMAN

Now you lis-ten here! It's
Kal-a-ma-zoo to
ev-er you please, they

worth it, my dear! There ain't man-y who are as luck-y as you are when
Tim-buck-in'-tu, Pa-du-cah to Pel-ham, they'll die when you tell 'em that
fall to their knees. I ain't seen a fel-low who does-n't go jel-lo when

you're a Co-pa girl! It's the Co-pa-co-los-sal-ca-ba-na! It's the oy-
you're a Co-pa girl. Ev-'ry day finds your name in the pa-pers, ev-'ry night
you're a Co-pa girl. You'll be feel-in' as if you're De-li-lah leav-in' Sam-

ster and you're the pearl! _____
is a so - cial whirl. _____
son with - out a curl. _____
You'll be the new Si - gno - ra who's
You meet a Greek ex - plor - er, you're
They'll be

ooz - ing with au - ra when you're a Co - pa girl. ____
off to Bo - ra Bo - ra when you're a Co - pa girl. ____

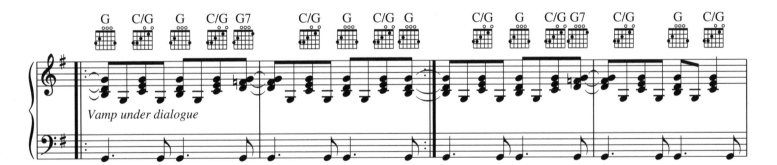

Vamp under dialogue

(Spoken:) ...Daggers! But being the lady you are, you just turn to them, smile and politely say,
(Spoken:) ...from Pittsburgh, PA." And he says, "Well, well, Gladys Murphy, you are a very beautiful woman." And I say softly,

"Drop dead, I'm a Copa girl!"
*"Bet your royal heinie – I'm a
Copa Girl!"*

From

What-

mak-ing room for a   new chap-ter in the Tor-ah

when   you're   a   Co - pa

girl! _____

D.S. al Coda

CODA

MAN WANTED

Music by BARRY MANILOW
Lyric by BRUCE SUSSMAN and JACK FELDMAN

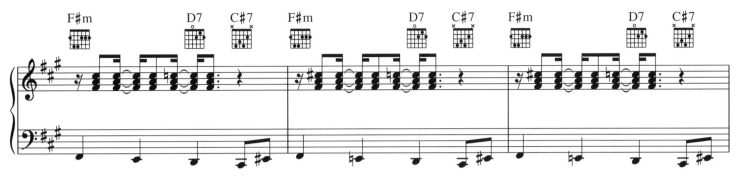

Man _____ want-ed, one han-dy man want-ed,

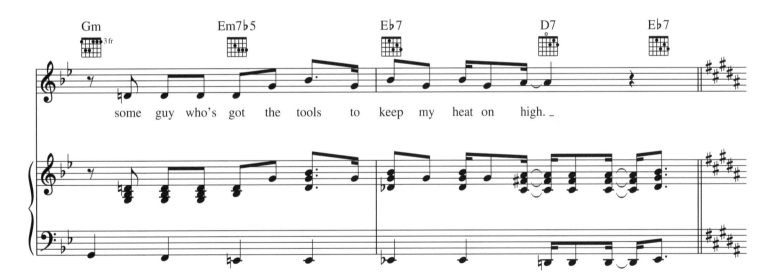

some guy who's got the tools to keep my heat on high. _

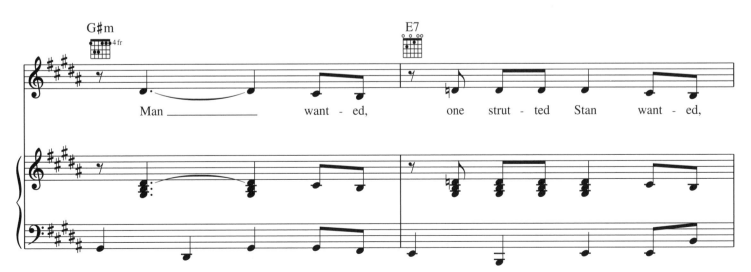

Man _____ want-ed, one strut-ted Stan want-ed,

LOLA

Music by BARRY MANILOW
Lyric by BRUCE SUSSMAN and JACK FELDMAN

Segue: "Who Needs to Dream"

WHO NEEDS TO DREAM

Music by BARRY MANILOW and ARTIE BUTLER
Lyric by BRUCE SUSSMAN and JACK FELDMAN

You were in my dreams, al-ways in my dreams. That was

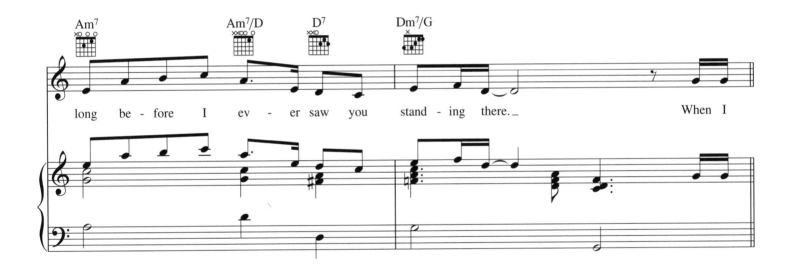

long be-fore I ev-er saw you stand-ing there. When I

felt a - fraid of the choice I made, I would
fan - ta - sy you be - lieved in me, and as

close my eyes and hope my dreams would com - fort me. __ But now I´m free. __
long as you were there then I be - lieved in me. __ Now sud - den - ly, __

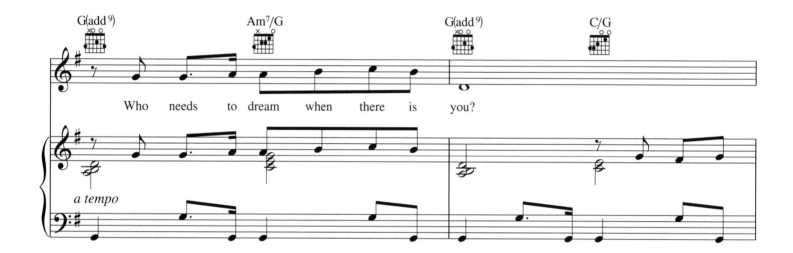

Who needs to dream when there is you?

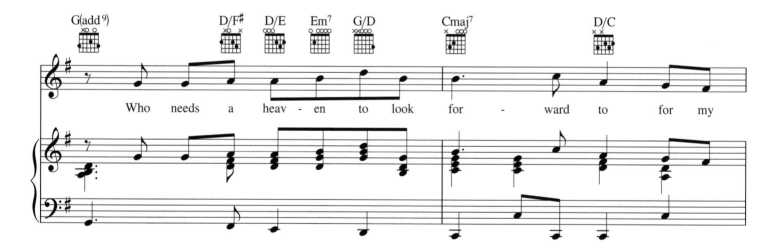

Who needs a heav - en to look for - ward to for my

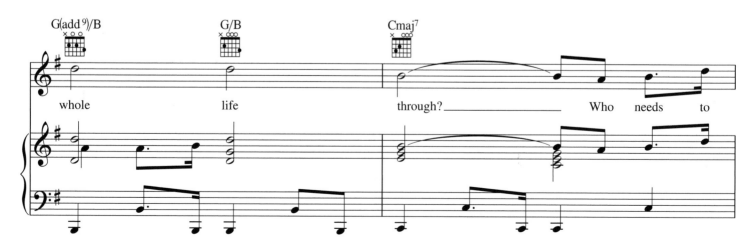

whole life through? _____ Who needs to

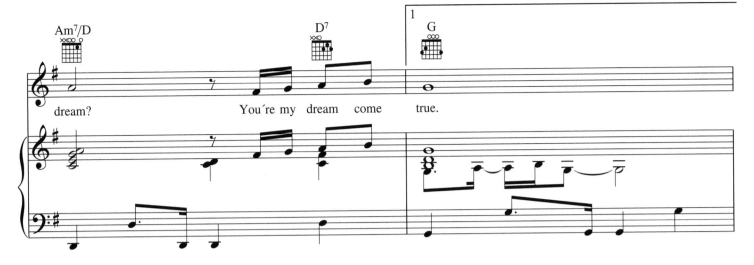

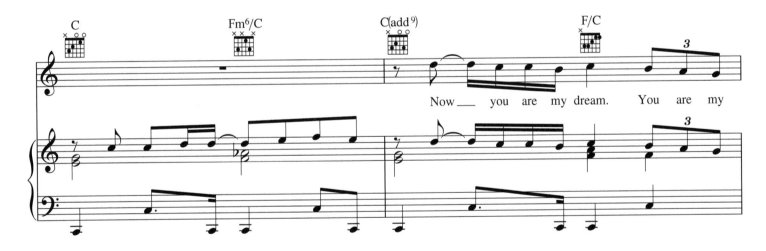

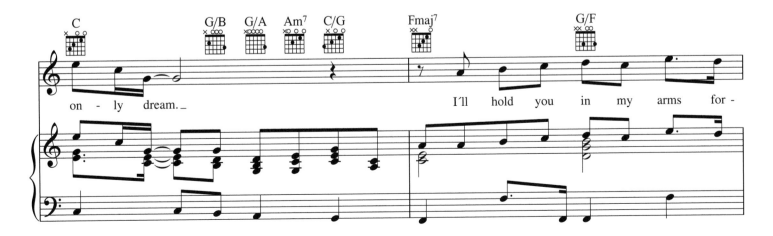

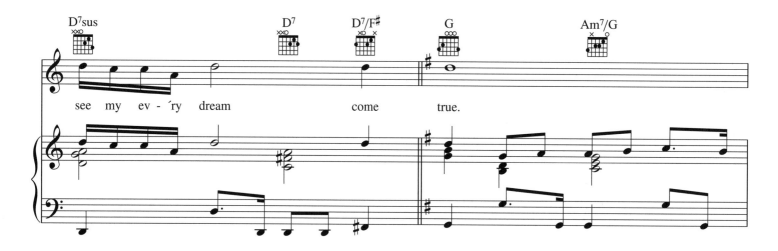

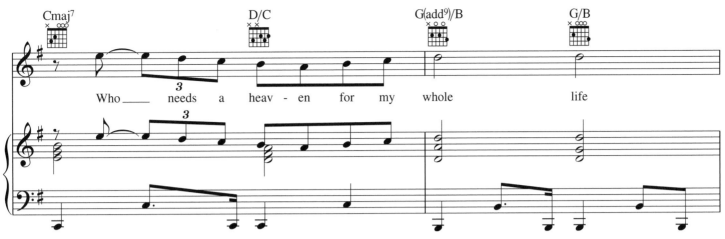

Who ____ needs a heav-en for my whole life

through? _____ Who needs to dream? You're my dream come

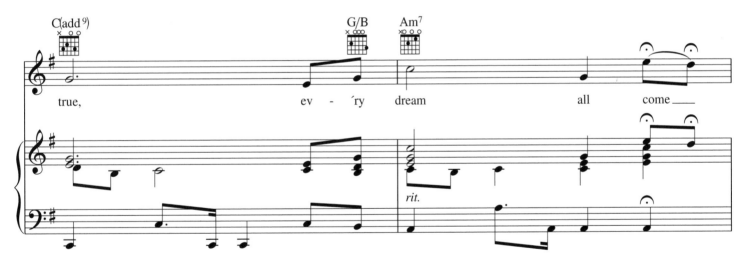

true, ev-'ry dream all come ____

true. My dream come true.

a tempo *rit.*

I GOTTA BE BAD

Music by BARRY MANILOW
Lyric by BRUCE SUSSMAN

Fast March, in 2

While the boys were off to war, we were left to mind the store. We kept the land of free-dom hum-ming shore to shore. Now the

42

BOLERO DE AMOR

Music by BARRY MANILOW
Lyric by BRUCE SUSSMAN and JACK FELDMAN

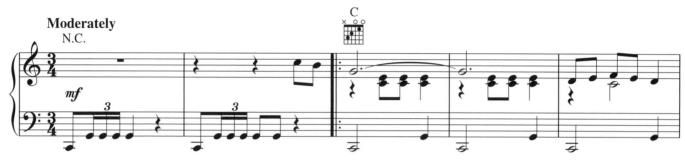

RICO: There are times you live as if in a dream, drawn by your heart to a dis- tant
(2nd time)

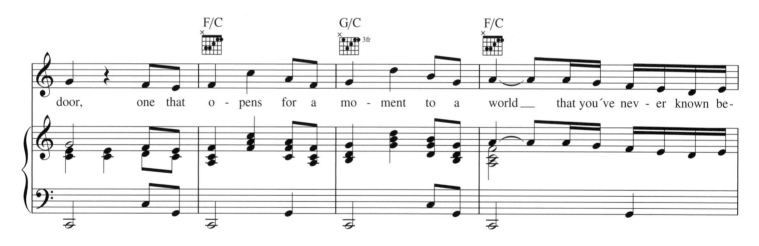

door, one that o- pens for a mo- ment to a world___ that you´ve nev- er known be-

fore. Were you real or were you part of a dream, call- ing to me from a- cross the

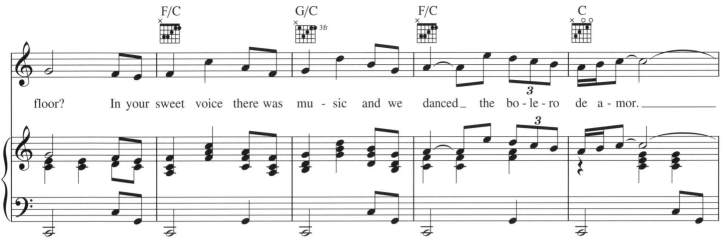

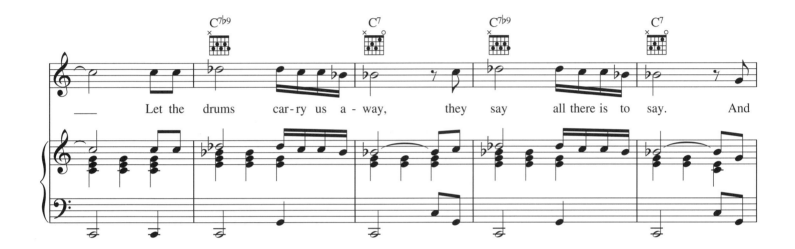

46

pas - sion soar like mu - sic in the spell of bo - le - ro de a - mor.____

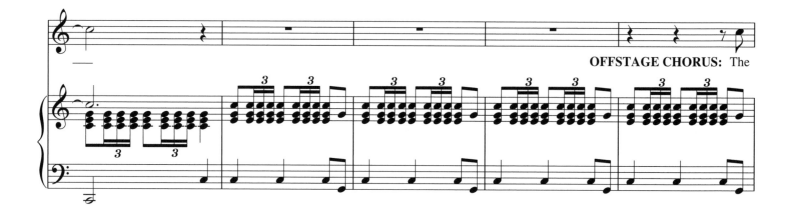

OFFSTAGE CHORUS: The

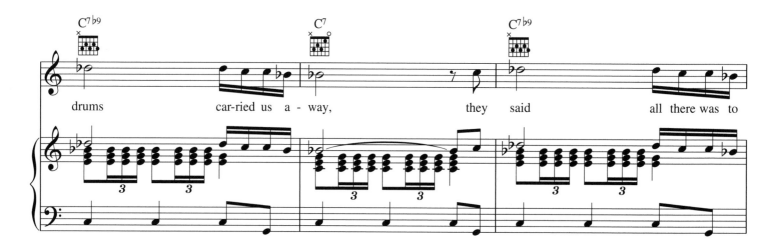

drums   car-ried us a - way,   they said   all there was to

say   and all____ too soon the night   be - comes the day   and

mag - i - cal mir - a - cle, **RICO:** there are times you live as if in a dream, drawn by your heart to a dis - tant

door. Trust your heart and take the mo - ment when you hear your bo - le - ro

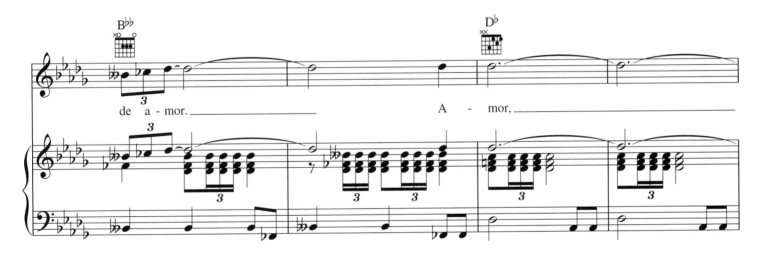

de a - mor. A - mor,

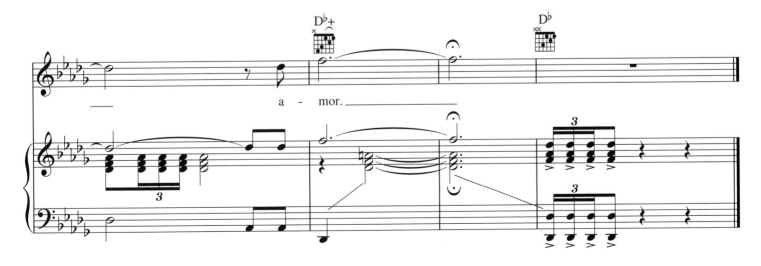

a - mor.

WELCOME TO HAVANA/
AYE CARAMBA

Music by BARRY MANILOW
Lyric by BRUCE SUSSMAN and JACK FELDMAN

WELCOME TO HAVANA

Wel-come to Ha-van - a! _____ Wel-come to Ha-van - a!

_____ Wel-come to Ha-van - a, where the world is on _ va - ca-tion.

AYE CARAMBA

WHO AM I KIDDING

Music by BARRY MANILOW
Lyric by BRUCE SUSSMAN and JACK FELDMAN

SAM: Ha - van - a, Ha - van - a, Ha - van - a freak-in' Cu - ba.

The kid is head-ing for a crash. He'll run in-to Cas-tel-li there, they'll

shoot him in the bel - ly there, they'll cut him up and stuff him in the trash. Ho - ly cow! Ha-

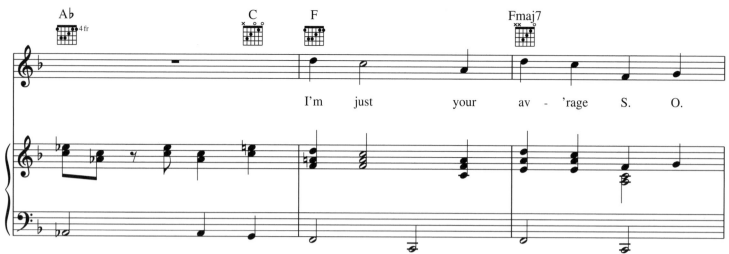

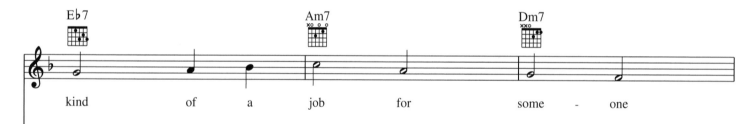

* Pronounced "i-yun."

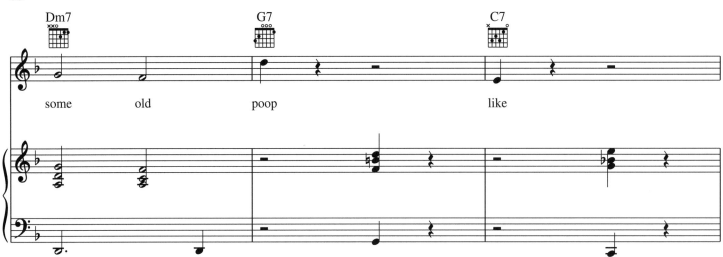

some old poop like

me.

GLADYS: Cas -

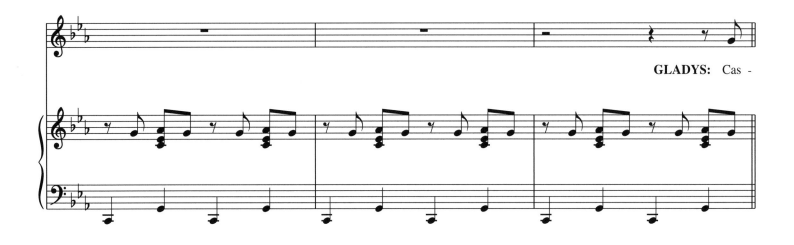

tel - li, Cas - tel - li, you've got - ta stop Cas - tel - li. The kid don't know him like we

like me.
Aw!

ALL BUT SAM: Looks like we got our - selves a

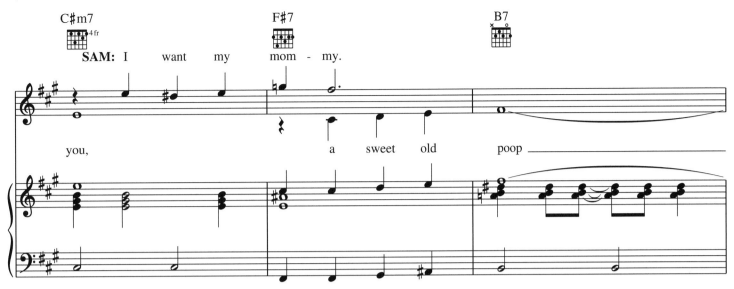

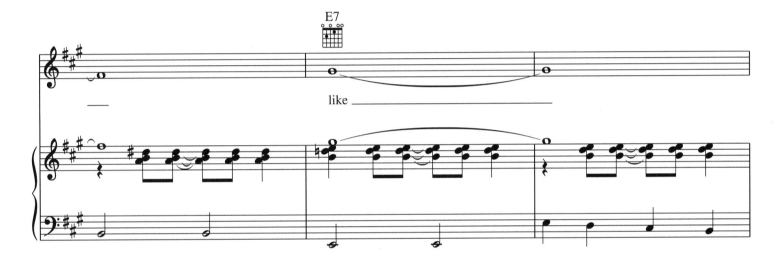

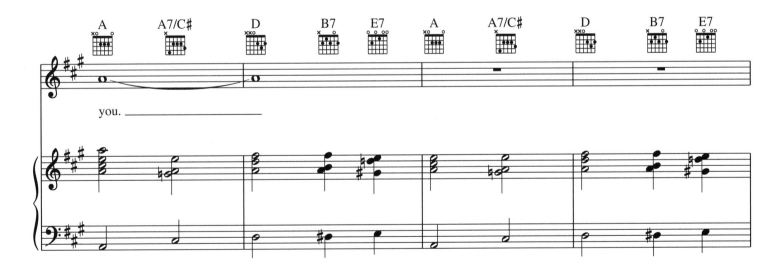

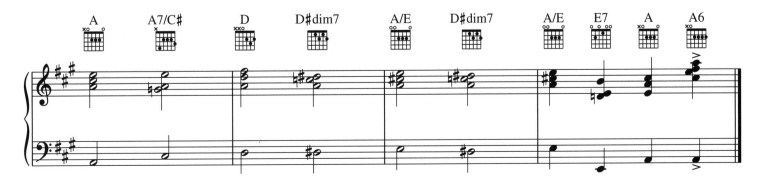

WHO AM I KIDDING
(Reprise)

Music by BARRY MANILOW
Lyric by BRUCE SUSSMAN and JACK FELDMAN

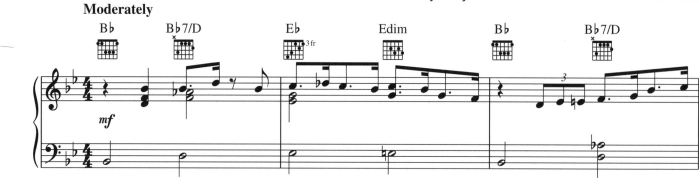

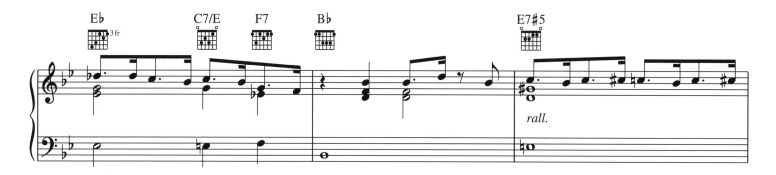

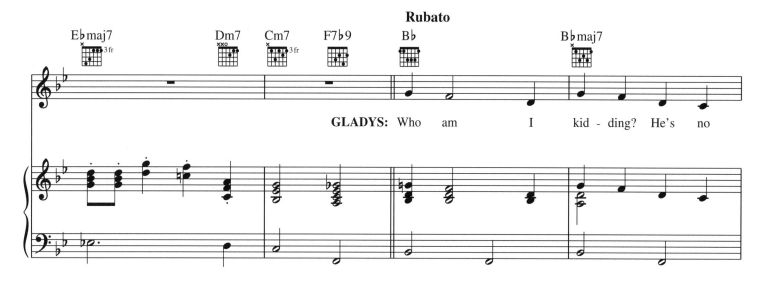

GLADYS: Who am I kid-ding? He's no

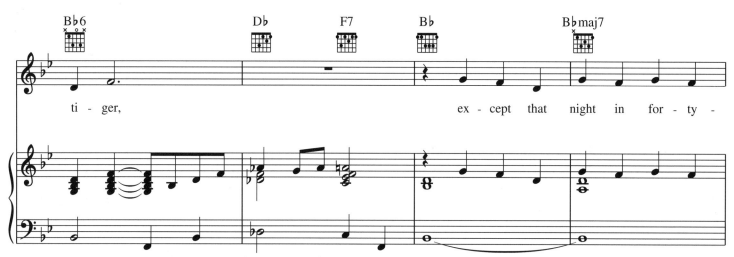

ti - ger, ex - cept that night in for - ty -

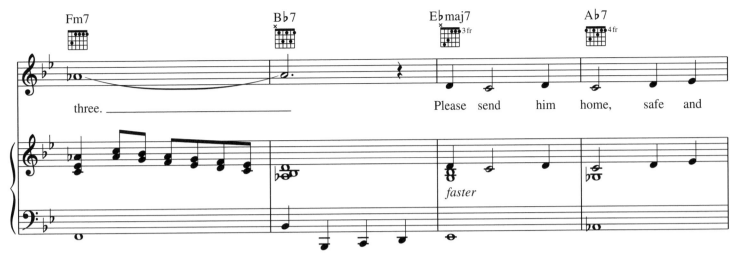

three. _____ Please send him home, safe and

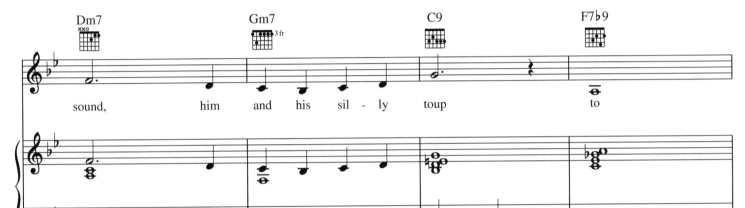

sound, him and his sil - ly toup to

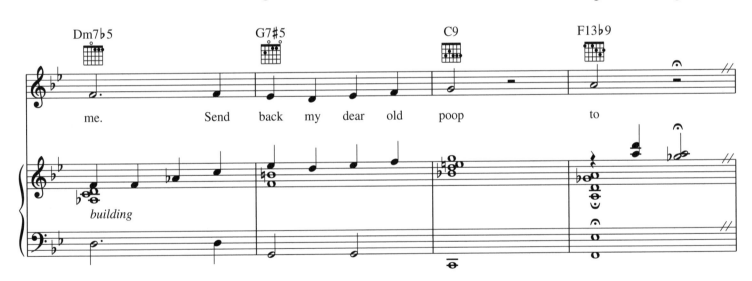

me. Send back my dear old poop to

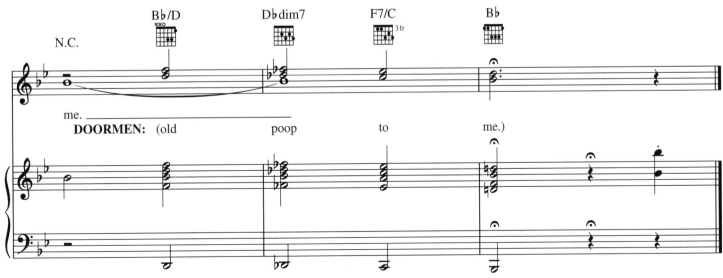

me. _____
DOORMEN: (old poop to me.)

THIS CAN'T BE REAL

Music by BARRY MANILOW
Lyric by BRUCE SUSSMAN and JACK FELDMAN

Moderately

LOLA: This can't be real as long as I love you.

How could this ev-er be real, as long as you're

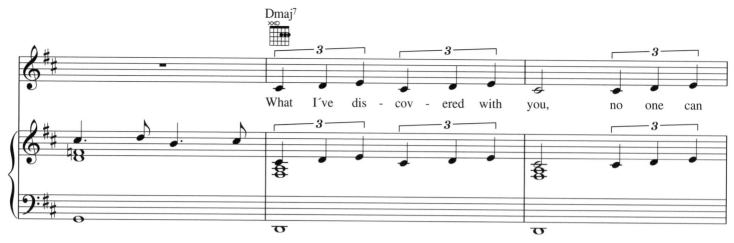

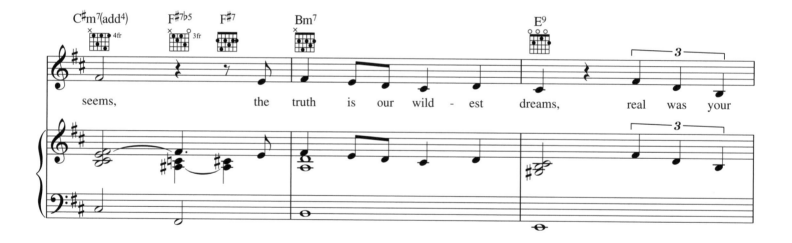

STEPHEN:
This can't be real, _____ so why do I love her? _____

I know that this can't be real, still she is

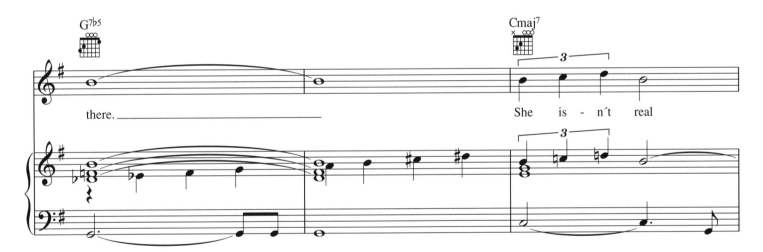

there. _____ She is -n't real

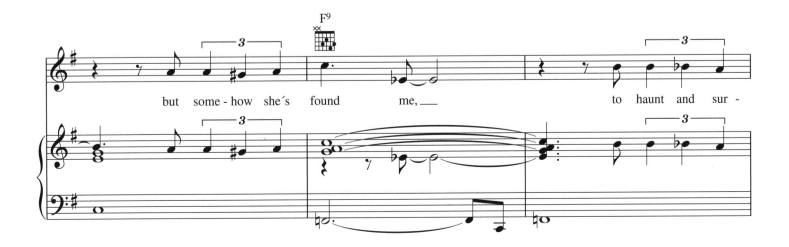

but some - how she's found me, _____ to haunt and sur -

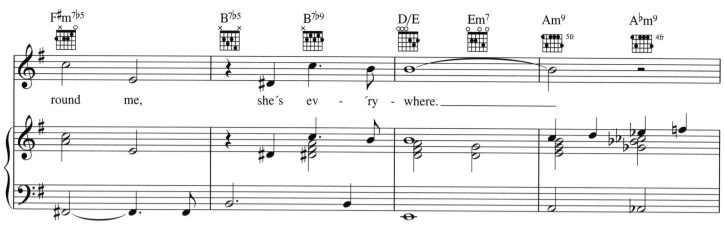

round me, she´s ev - ´ry - where._____

This is - n´t true, it´s on - ly il - lu - sion,_____

what I´ve dis - cov - ered with you is just an i - deal._____ You´re

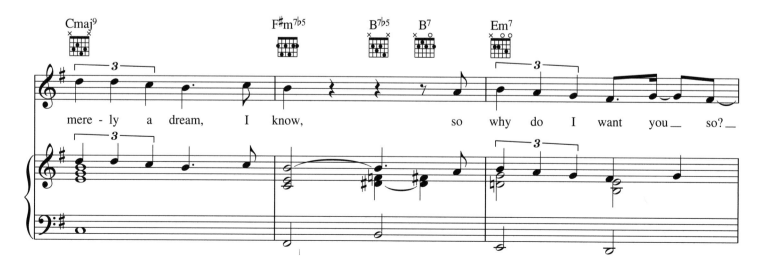

mere - ly a dream, I know, so why do I want you__ so?__

Is it be - cause, on - ly be - cause, this can't be

real, this can't be real.

STEPHEN & LOLA: Love is what's true, _____ the rest is il - lu - sion,

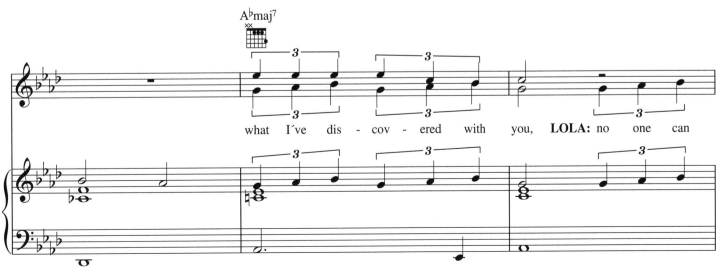

what I've dis - cov - ered with you, **LOLA:** no one can

72

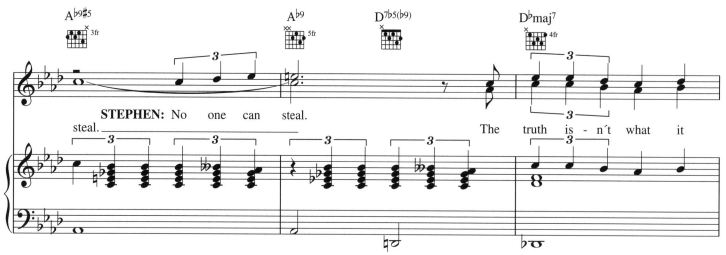

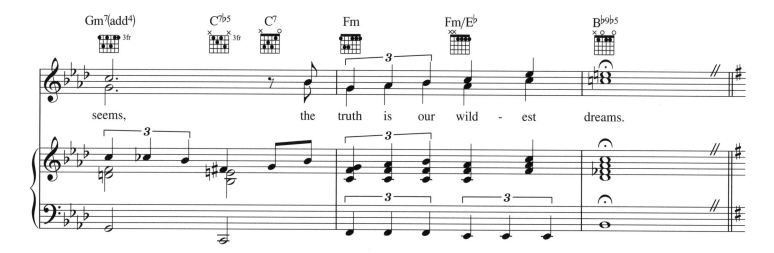

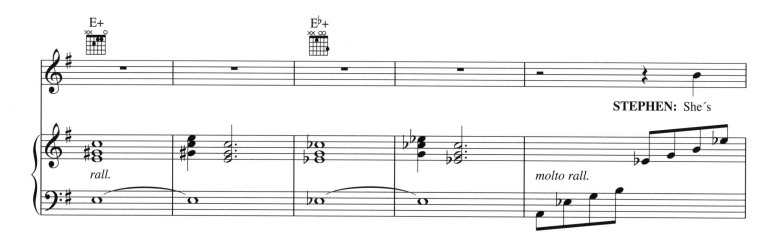

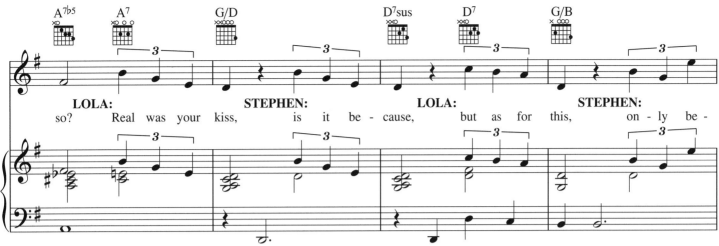

LOLA: STEPHEN: LOLA: STEPHEN:
so? Real was your kiss, is it be - cause,   but as for this,   on - ly be -

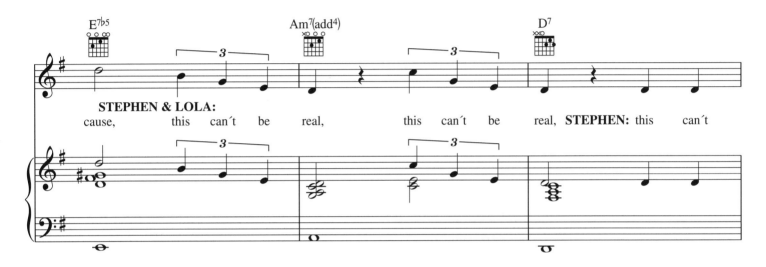

STEPHEN & LOLA:
cause,   this can't be   real,   this can't be   real, STEPHEN: this   can't

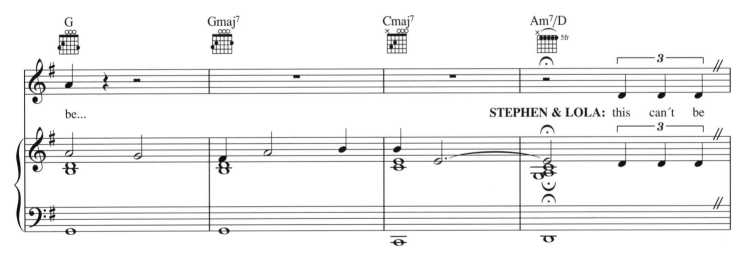

be...   STEPHEN & LOLA: this can't be

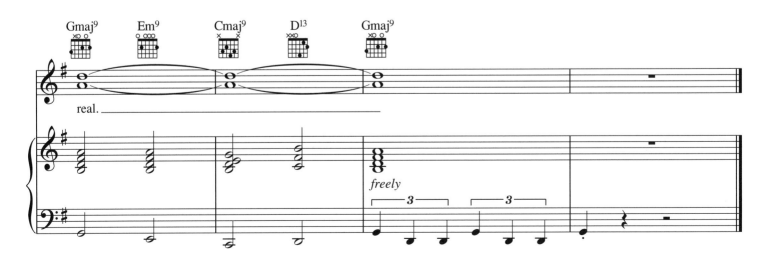

real. _____

freely

EL BRAVO

Music by BARRY MANILOW
Lyric by BRUCE SUSSMAN and JACK FELDMAN

Brightly

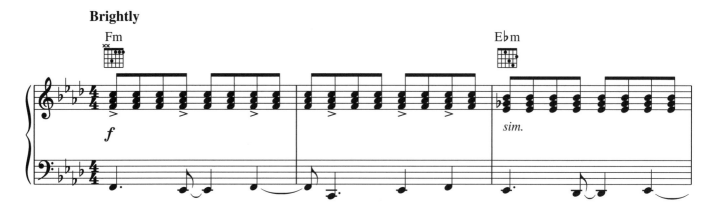

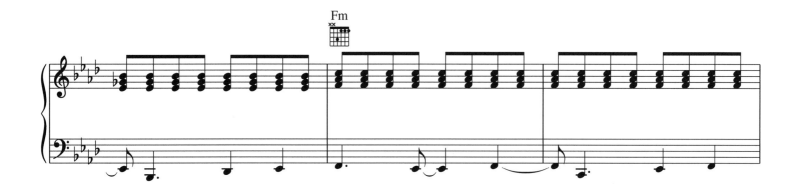

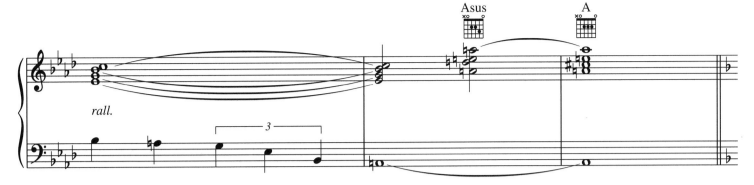

Tempo I

PIRATE CAPTAIN: *Pirates, have your way with her!*

and the meek and the soon

ALL:

to be dead, and the sad and the sick. Dar - ling, quick, it's the nick of

LOLA:

time.

PIRATES: El Bra - vo, **ALL:** El

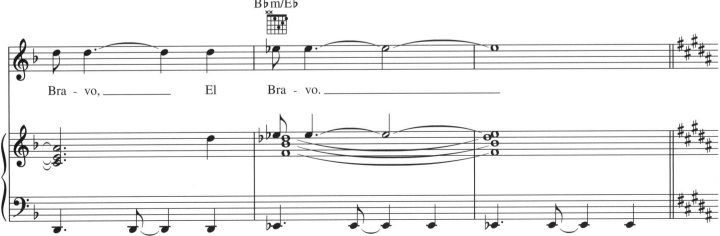

Bra - vo, El Bra - vo.

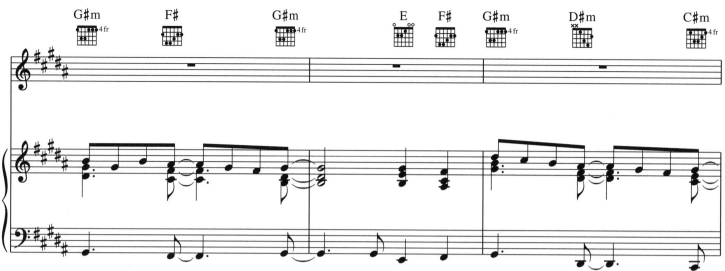

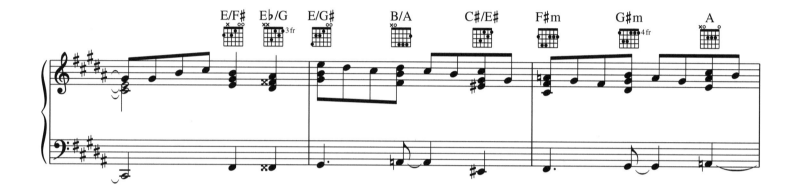

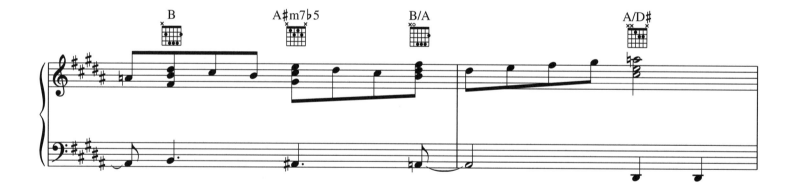

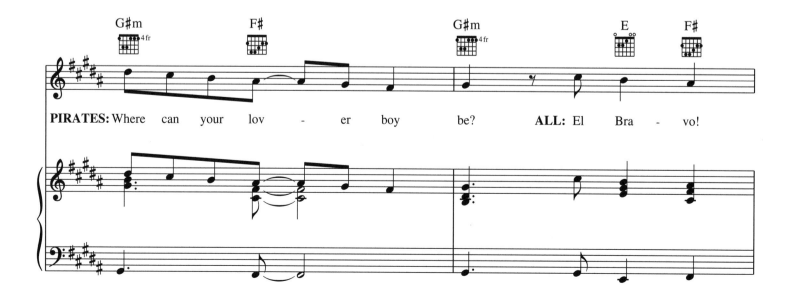

PIRATES: Where can your lov - er boy be? **ALL:** El Bra - vo!

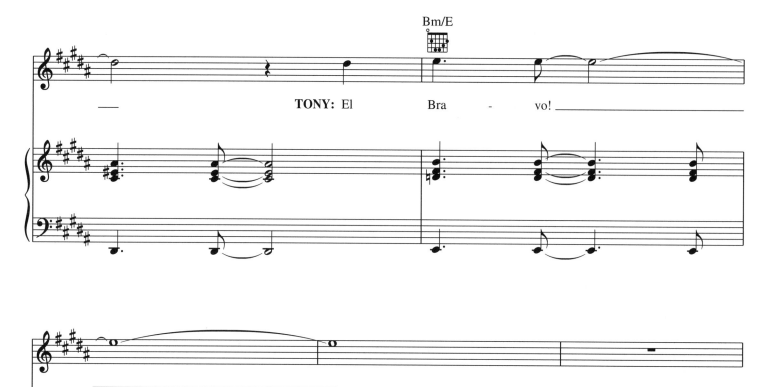

TONY: El Bra - vo!

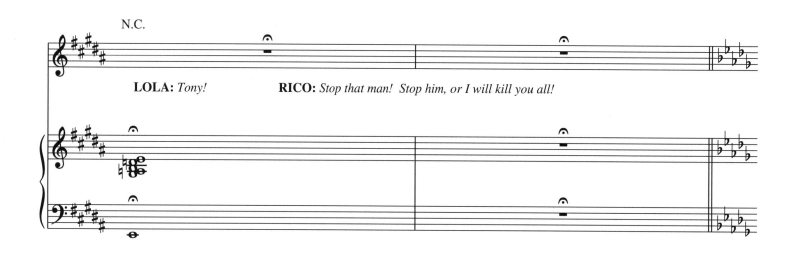

LOLA: *Tony!*   RICO: *Stop that man! Stop him, or I will kill you all!*

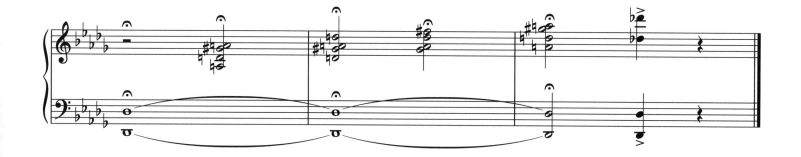

COPACABANA
(At the Copa)

Music by BARRY MANILOW
Lyric by BRUCE SUSSMAN and JACK FELDMAN

Moderately, with a Latin feel

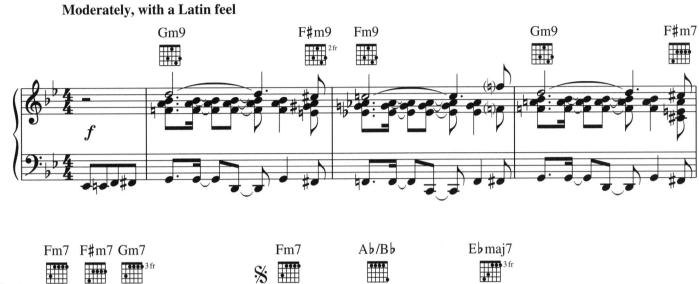

Her name was Lo - la; __ she was a show - girl __ with yel - low
Ri - co; __ he wore a dia - mond, __ he was es -
Lo - la; __ she was a show - girl, __ but that was

feath - ers in her hair and a dress cut down to there. She would Mer -
cort - ed to his chair, he saw Lo - la danc - ing there. And when she
thir - ty years a - go when they used to have a show. Now it's a

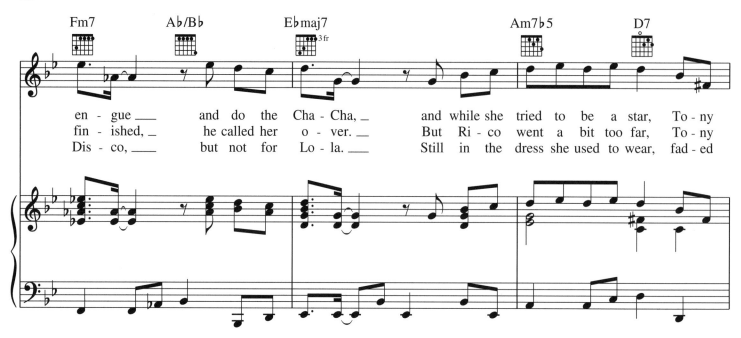

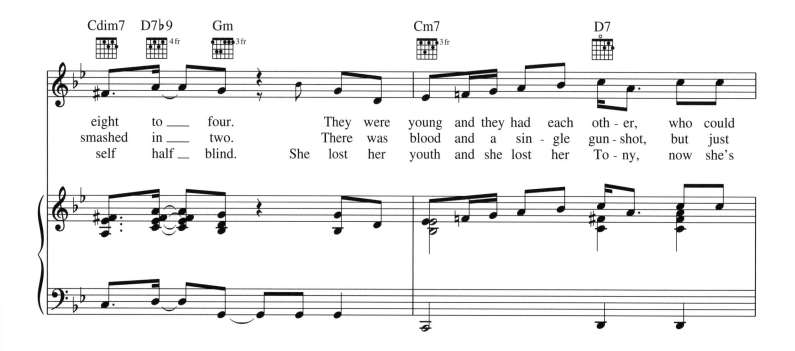

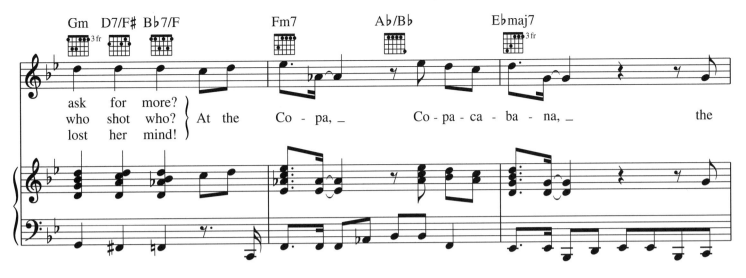

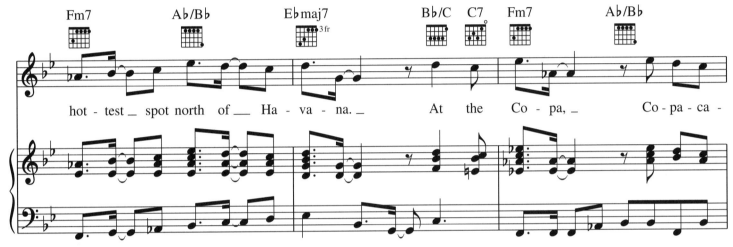

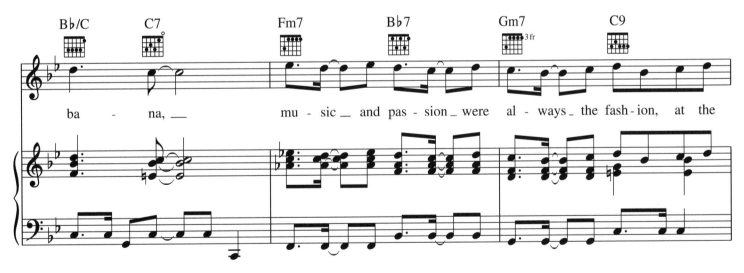

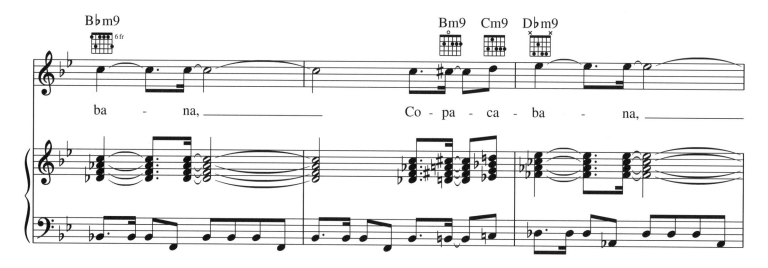

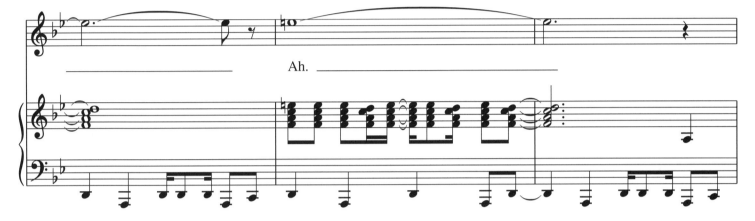

Instrumental solo ad lib.